# Scroll Saw
# Basket Weave
# Projects

## 12 advanced authentic-looking baskets

by
John Nelson
and
William Guimond

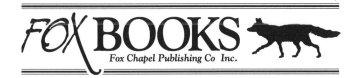

Fox Chapel Publishing Co., Inc.
1970 Broad Street
East Petersburg, PA 17520

# Table of Contents

Copyright © 1998 Fox Chapel Publishing Company Inc.

Publisher:              Alan Giagnocavo
Project Editor:         Ayleen Stellhorn
Desktop Specialist:     Linda L. Eberly, Eberly Designs Inc.

ISBN # 1-56523-103-1

To order your copy of this book,
please send check or money order
for $9.95 plus $2.50 shipping to:
Fox Books Orders
1970 Broad Street
East Petersburg, PA 17520

*Try your favorite book supplier first!*

We wish to thank Colette Guimond for her beautiful lid design (last project), Joyce Nelson for typing the book manuscript and Alan Giagnocavo and the staff at Fox Chapel Publishing Company, Inc. Without their help this book could not have been published.

# Basic Instructions

The basket patterns included in this book are only a beginning. Use your imagination to create hundreds of other designs of you own: add layers to increase the height of your basket, use thicker or thinner layers for different effects, enlarge or reduce the pattern for a particular need, use different kinds of wood to change the look of your basket. In doing this, you will create a basket that is truly *your* design. The combinations you can use are endless.

### Finishing Your Basket

We recommend leaving the finished baskets with no finish at all on them, just their natural wood. If, however, you wish to stain or apply a satin finish coat of varnish to your basket, use any available commercial stain or varnish product that you would apply on any other wood working project. Apply per instructions on the container. For ease, try to use a spray top coat, it will speed up your work.

### Suggested Materials

As with all scroll saw projects, always use high quality, knot-free wood. Recommended woods for baskets are aspen, basswood or poplar. They are hardwoods and cut easily on the scroll saw. Most soft woods are not recommended because they have little "character." To add trim or color variations use mahogany, cherry, maple or red oak. For example, you may choose to use a maple wood for the base, top rim and handle, then use a mahogany wood for the levels of the basket.

# 1 Pencil- Pen Holder

## with optional canister lid

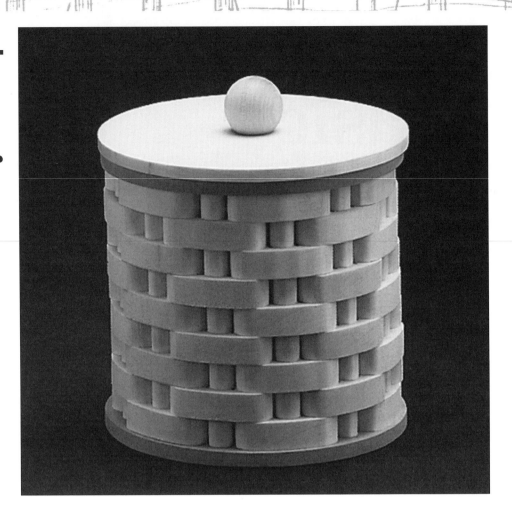

**Assembly View**

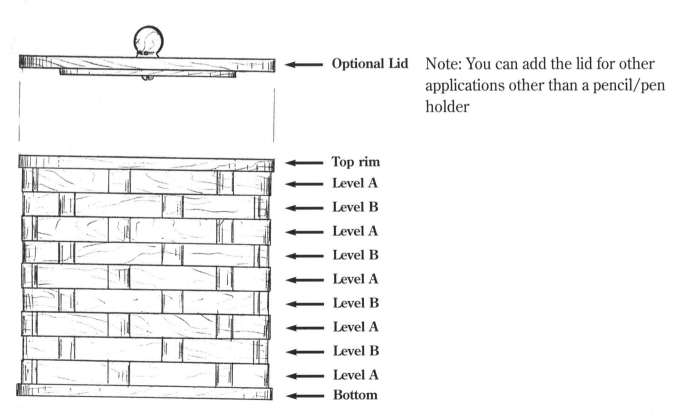

Optional Lid

Note: You can add the lid for other applications other than a pencil/pen holder

Top rim
Level A
Level B
Level A
Level B
Level A
Level B
Level A
Level B
Level A
Bottom

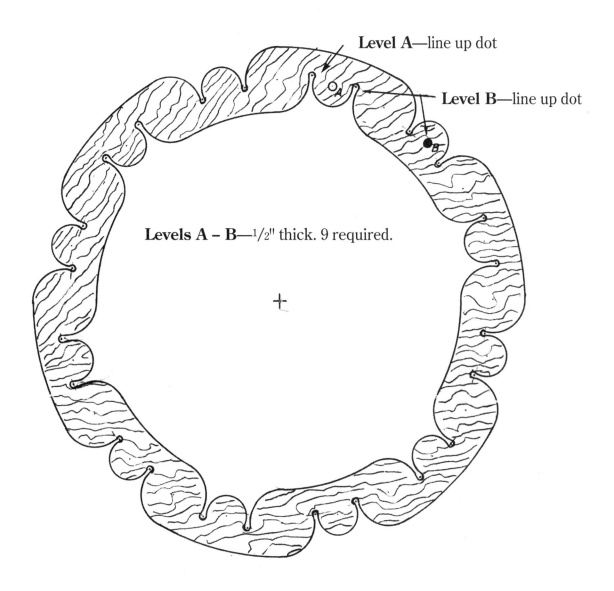

Level A—line up dot

Level B—line up dot

Levels A – B—$^1/_2$" thick. 9 required.

**Cut out as shown.**
**Line up dot A with dot B to get a *weave* affect.**
To make a taller basket add more levels.

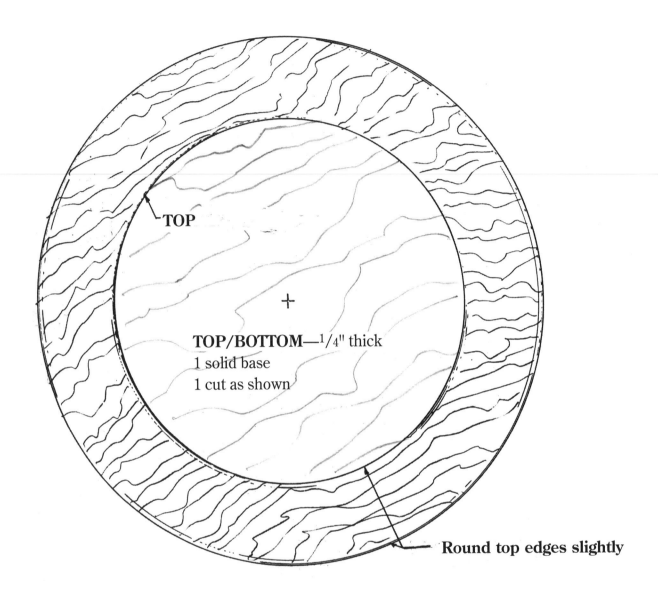

**TOP**

**TOP/BOTTOM**—$1/4''$ thick
1 solid base
1 cut as shown

**Round top edges slightly**

For contrast, use a different wood than body (levels).
See photo of basket.

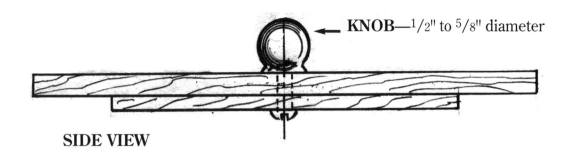

KNOB—$1/2''$ to $5/8''$ diameter

**SIDE VIEW**

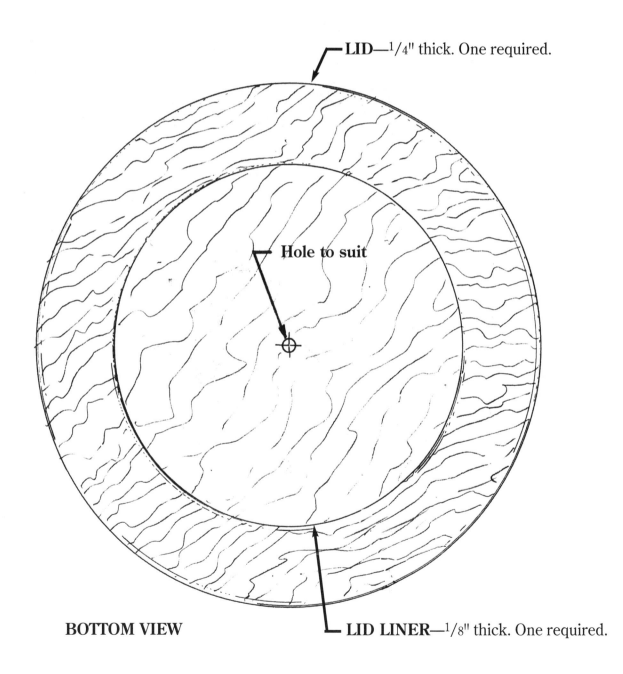

LID—$1/4''$ thick. One required.

Hole to suit

**BOTTOM VIEW**

LID LINER—$1/8''$ thick. One required.

# 2 Planter Basket

**accepts standard 3 inch clay pots**

Note: Optional top, less pots can be made. See pattern for top.

## Assembly View

3 inch clay pot. Two required.

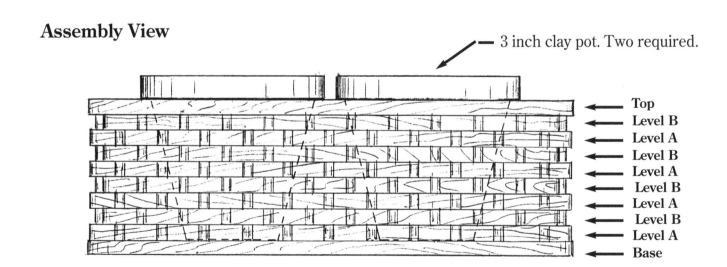

Top
Level B
Level A
Level B
Level A
Level B
Level A
Level B
Level A
Base

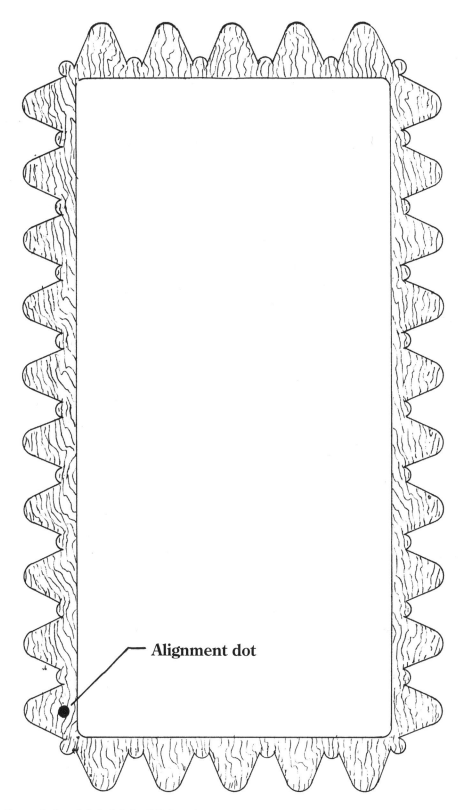

Alignment dot

Level A—1/4" thick. Make 4.

**Alignment dot**

**Level B**—$1/4''$ thick. Make 4.

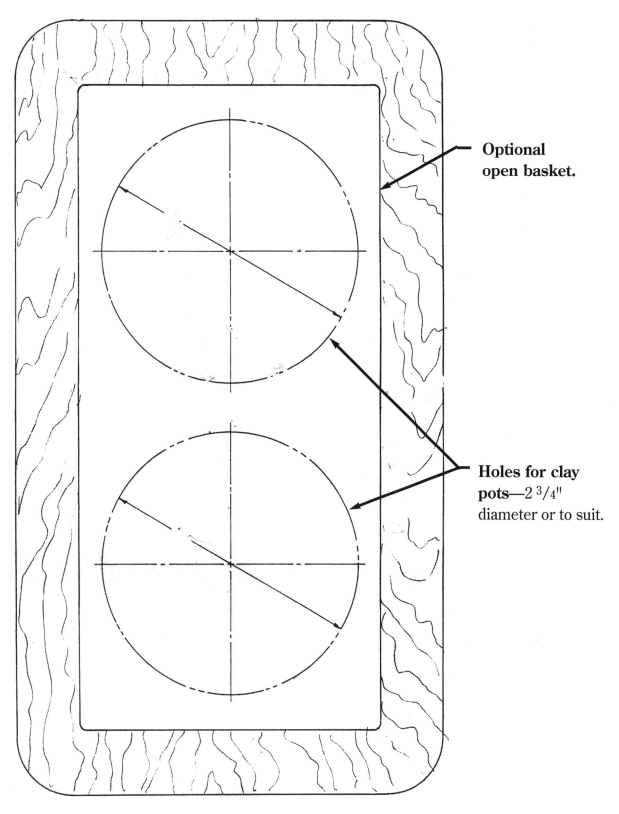

Optional
open basket.

Holes for clay
pots—2 3/4"
diameter or to suit.

**TOP**—1/4" thick. Make 4.

Round edges slightly.

**BASE**—1/4" thick. Make 1.

# 3 Tissue Box

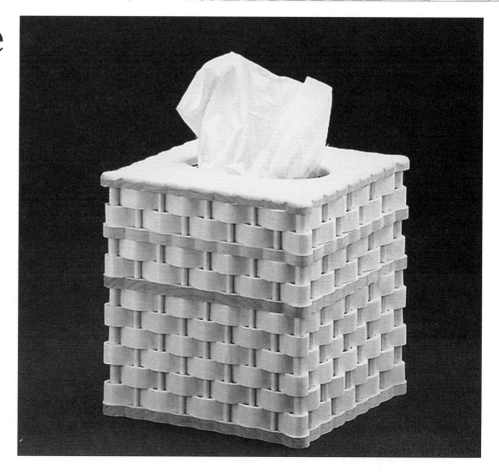

## Assembly View

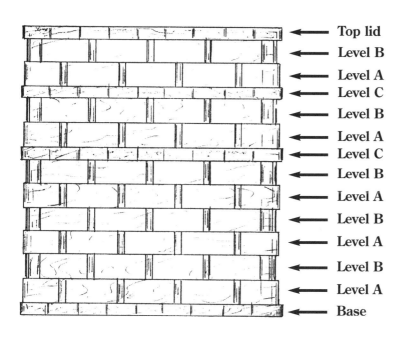

- Top lid
- Level B
- Level A
- Level C
- Level B
- Level A
- Level C
- Level B
- Level A
- Level B
- Level A
- Level B
- Level A
- Base

This tissue box can be painted or stained to fit into any decor in any room.

Line up dot.

CUT OUT

**Level A**—$1/2''$ thick. Make 5.

**Line up dot.**

CUT OUT

**Level B**—$1/2''$ thick. Make 5.

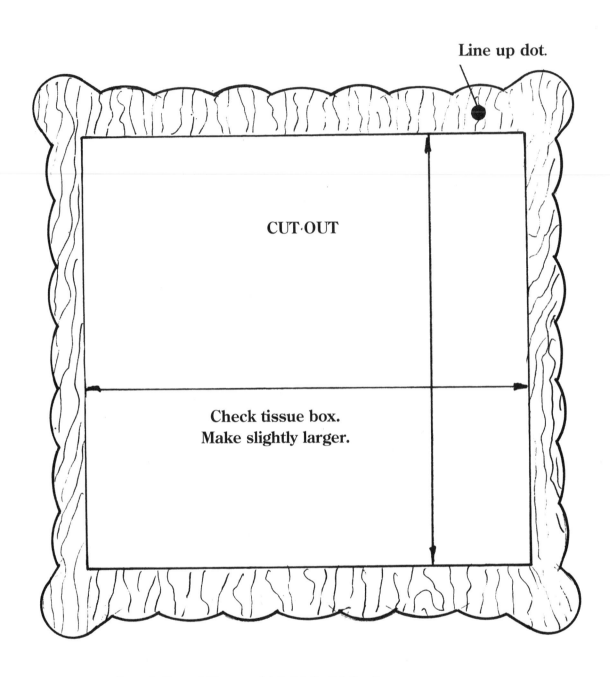

Line up dot.

CUT·OUT

Check tissue box.
Make slightly larger.

**Level C and Base**—1/4" thick. Make 3.
(Use a different wood for contrast or paint
level C and base.)

**Line up dot.**

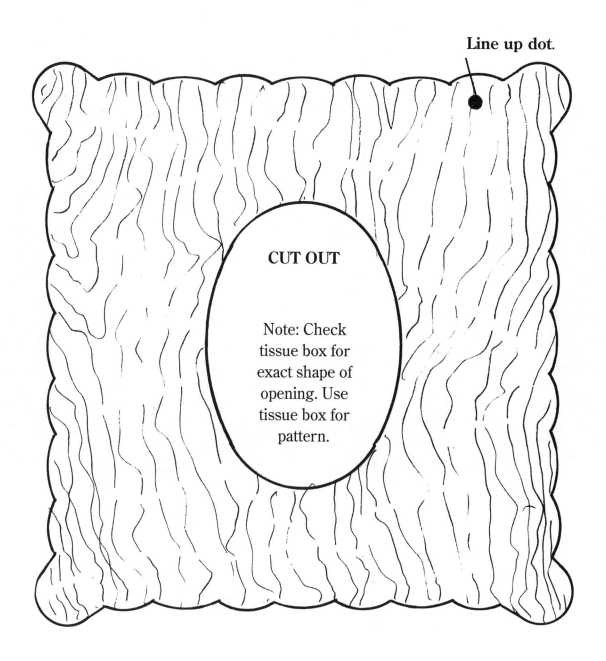

CUT OUT

Note: Check
tissue box for
exact shape of
opening. Use
tissue box for
pattern.

**Top Lid—**1/4" thick. Make 1.
(Use a different wood for contrast or paint
level C and base.)

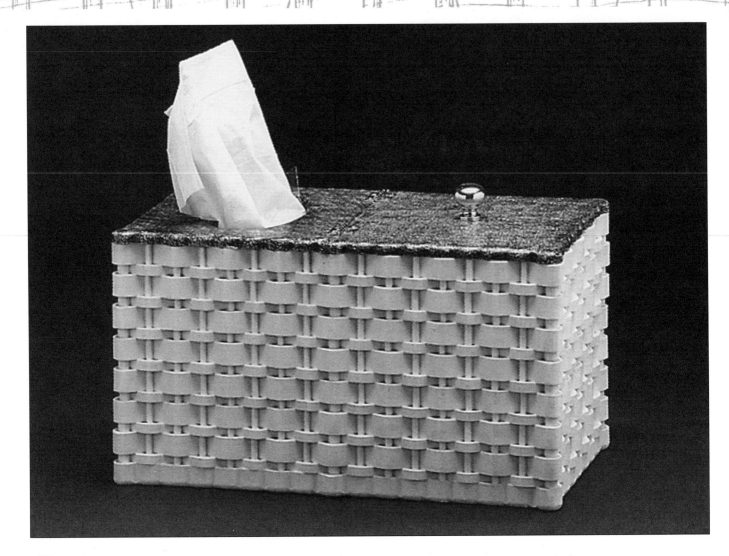

# 4 Tissue and Cotton Ball Basket

Note: This basket uses a combination of 1/2" wide weave and 1/4" wide weave. Top lid is "sponge" painted with a top coat of varnish. It is assembled exactly as previous baskets.

This tissue and cotton ball basket is used with the Q-tip® basket on page 21.

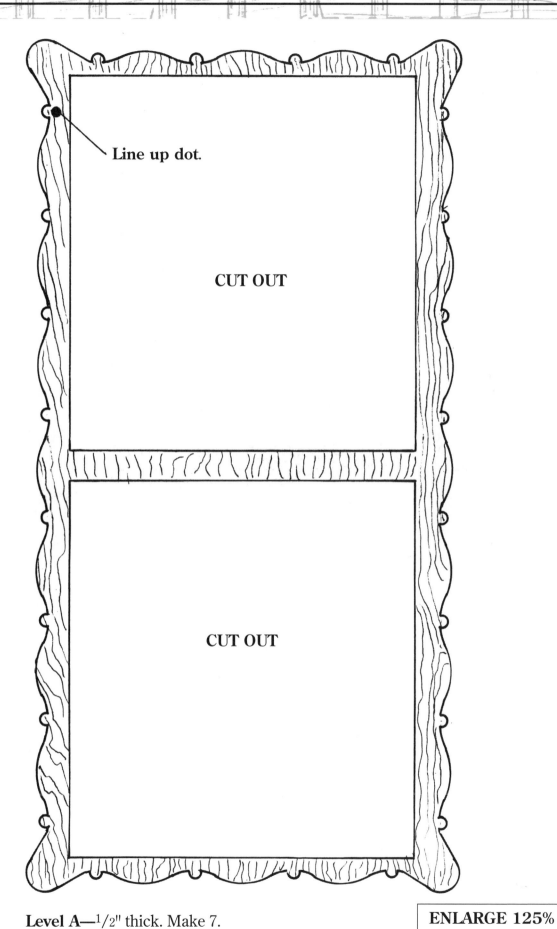

Line up dot.

CUT OUT

CUT OUT

Level A—1/2" thick. Make 7.

ENLARGE 125%

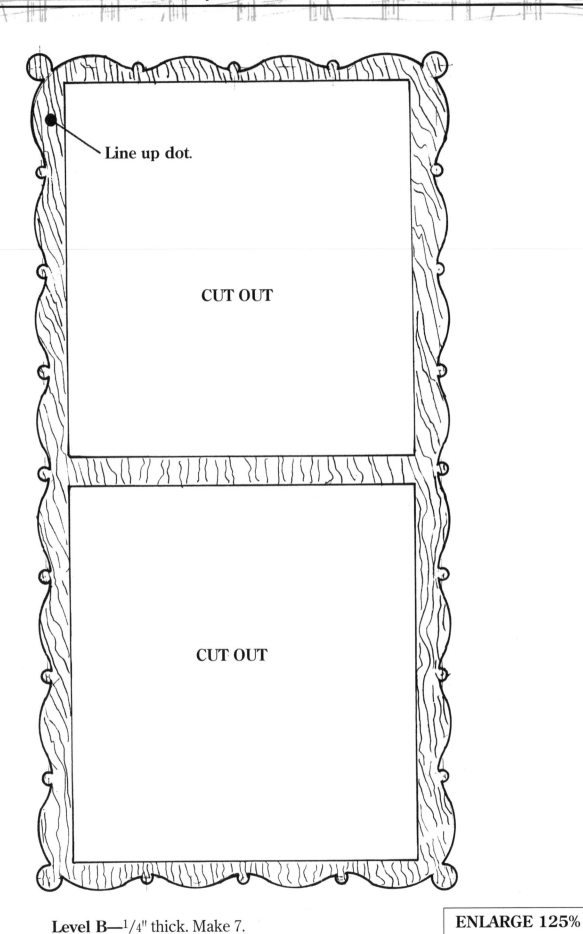

Line up dot.

CUT OUT

CUT OUT

Level B—¹/₄" thick. Make 7.

ENLARGE 125%

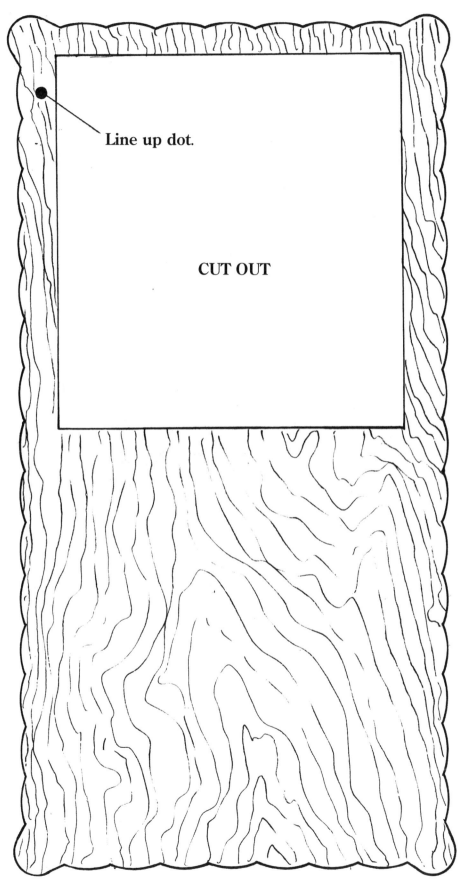

Line up dot.

CUT OUT

**Base**—1/2" thick. Make 1.

ENLARGE 125%

**Line up dot.**

**TOP
ASSEMBLY**

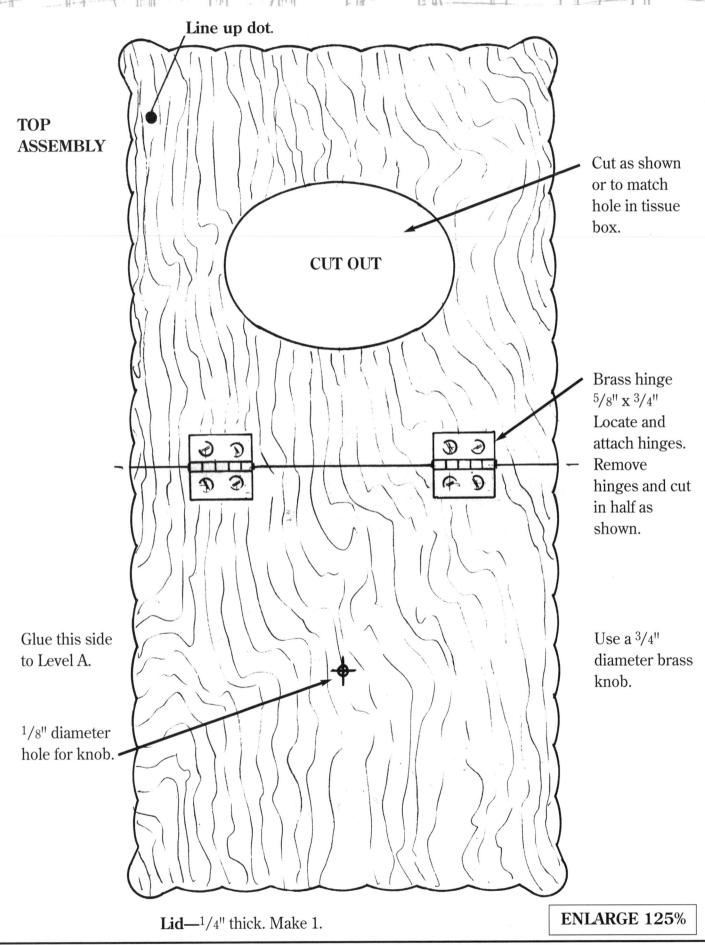

Cut as shown
or to match
hole in tissue
box.

**CUT OUT**

Brass hinge
$5/8''$ x $3/4''$
Locate and
attach hinges.
Remove
hinges and cut
in half as
shown.

Glue this side
to Level A.

Use a $3/4''$
diameter brass
knob.

$1/8''$ diameter
hole for knob.

**Lid**—$1/4''$ thick. Make 1.

**ENLARGE 125%**

# 5 Q-tip® Basket

This Q-tip® basket is designed to match the Tissue and Cotton Ball Basket on page 16. This basket also uses the combination of $1/2''$ wide weave and $1/4''$ wide weave. Top lid is sponge painted with a finish coat of varnish to match other basket on page 16. Assemble exactly as previous basket.

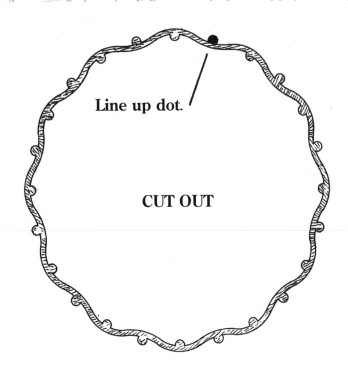

Line up dot.

CUT OUT

**Level A**—1/4" thick. Make 4.

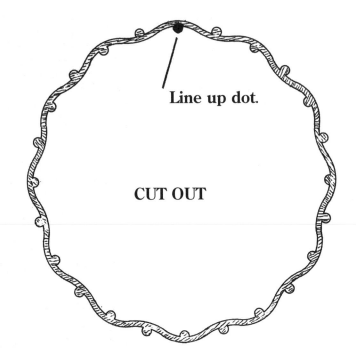

Line up dot.

CUT OUT

**Level B**—1/2" thick. Make 3.

**Lid**—1/4" thick. Make 1.

**Knob to suit.**

**Side view**

**Lid Liner**—1/8" thick. Make 1.

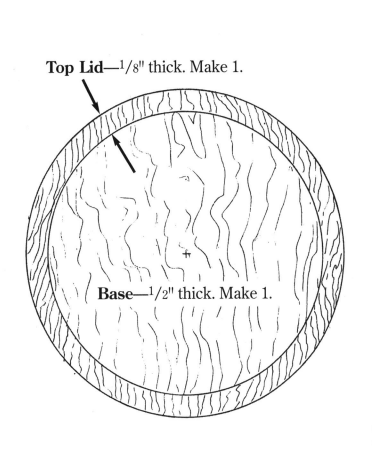

**Top Lid**—1/8" thick. Make 1.

**Base**—1/2" thick. Make 1.

1/8" diameter hole.

**LID ASSEMBLY**

**Bottom view**

# 6 Tulip Wall Basket

This basket has special vertical "stays" (made of a different wood). This gives a special "weave" affect and makes this wall box a woven basket.

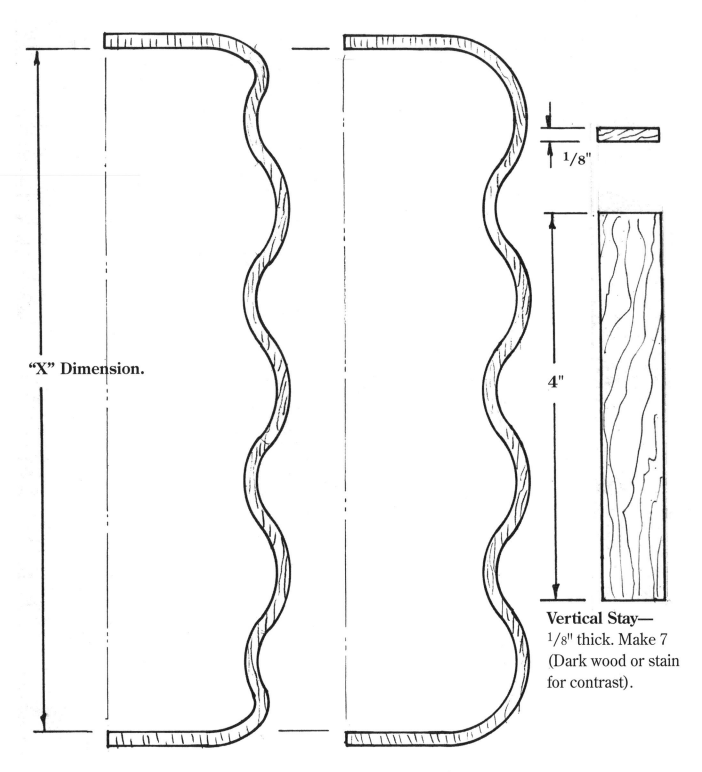

**"X" Dimension.**

1/8"

4"

**Vertical Stay—**
1/8" thick. Make 7
(Dark wood or stain
for contrast).

**Level A—**1/2" thick. Make 4.

**Level B—**1/2" thick. Make 4.

Note: Photo shows base and lip <u>straight</u>–no scallop edge

Add vertical stays as you glue levels together. (Fit or trim stays if necessary).

Optional scallop edge.

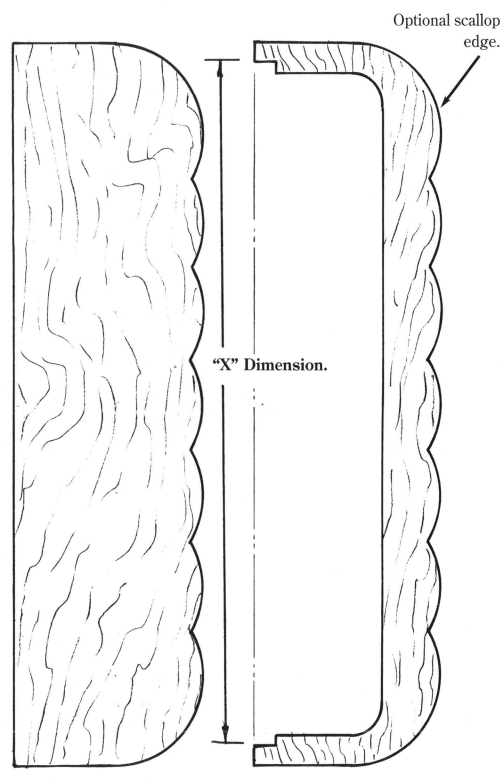

"X" Dimension.

**Base**—³/₈" thick. Make 1.          **Lip**—³/₈" thick. Make 1.

Note: Make sure dimension "X" in backboard fits with dimension "X" on Level A–B and lip.

ENLARGE 130%

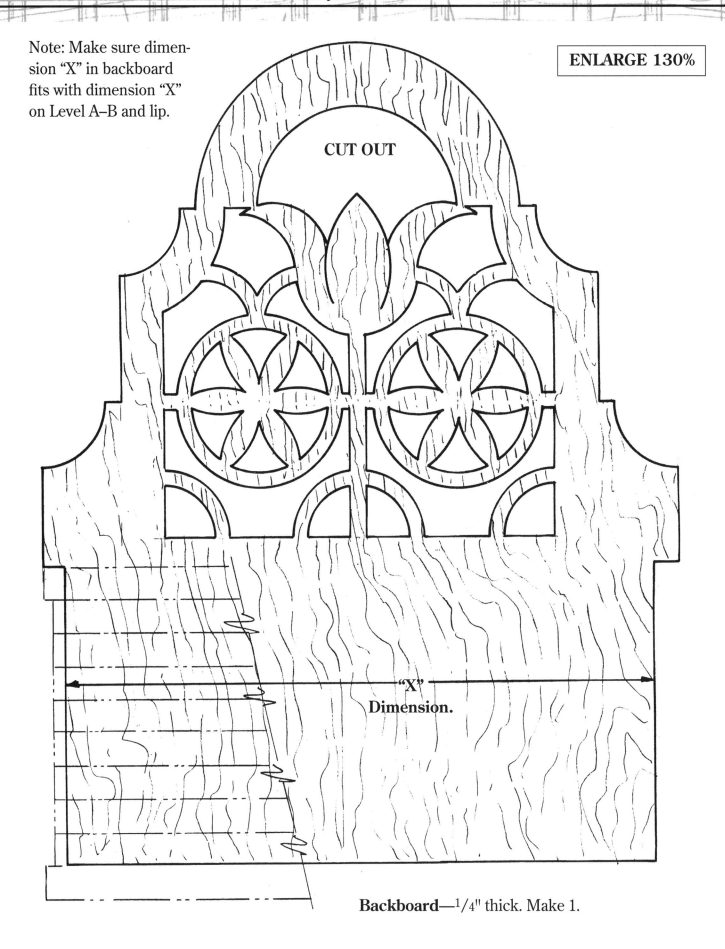

CUT OUT

"X" Dimension.

Backboard—1/4" thick. Make 1.

# 7 Tapered New Hampshire Basket

This is one of our most realistic woven baskets. The original woven basket was found in New Hampshire. This one will really fool your friends.

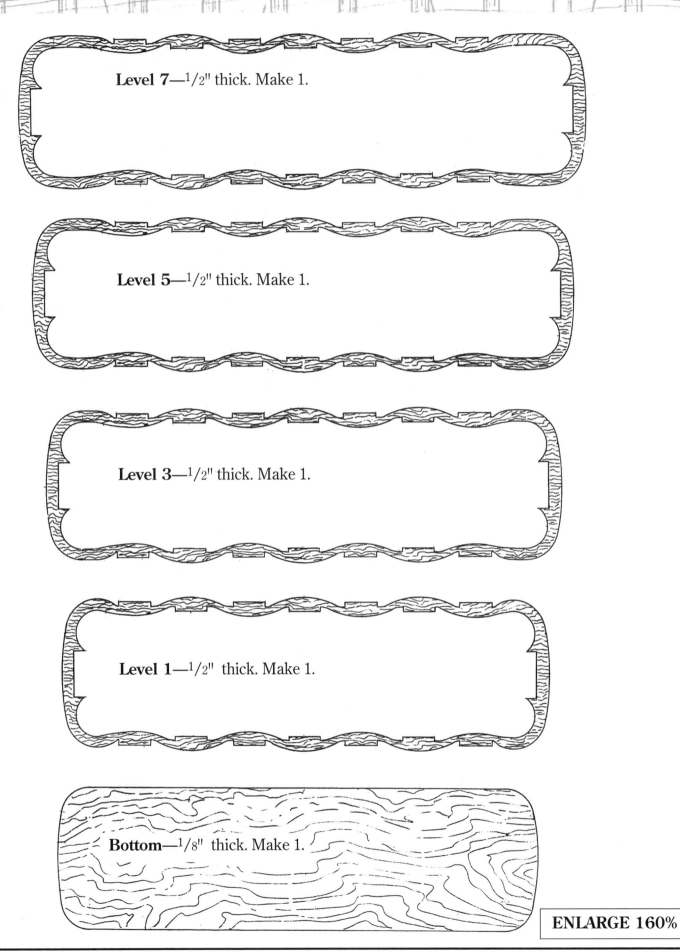

Level 7—1/2" thick. Make 1.

Level 5—1/2" thick. Make 1.

Level 3—1/2" thick. Make 1.

Level 1—1/2" thick. Make 1.

Bottom—1/8" thick. Make 1.

ENLARGE 160%

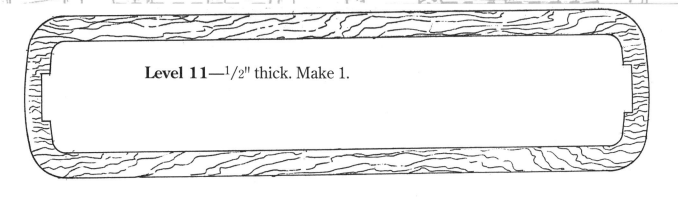

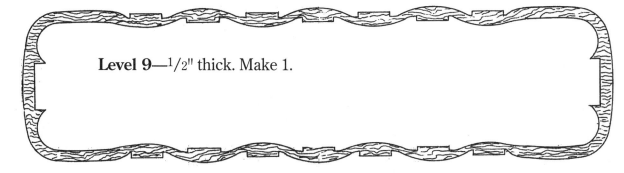

**Level 11**—1/2" thick. Make 1.

**Level 9**—1/2" thick. Make 1.

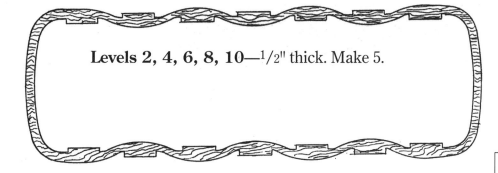

**Levels 2, 4, 6, 8, 10**—1/2" thick. Make 5.

**ENLARGE 160%**

**Handle brace**—3/4" thick. Make 1.

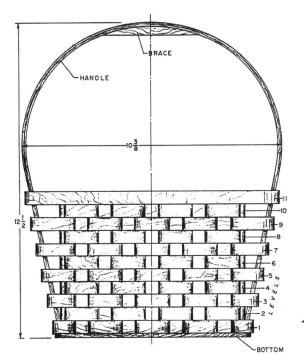

BRACE

HANDLE

10 3/8

12 1/2

11
10
9
8
7
6
5
4
3
2
1

LEVELS

BOTTOM

**Assembly View**

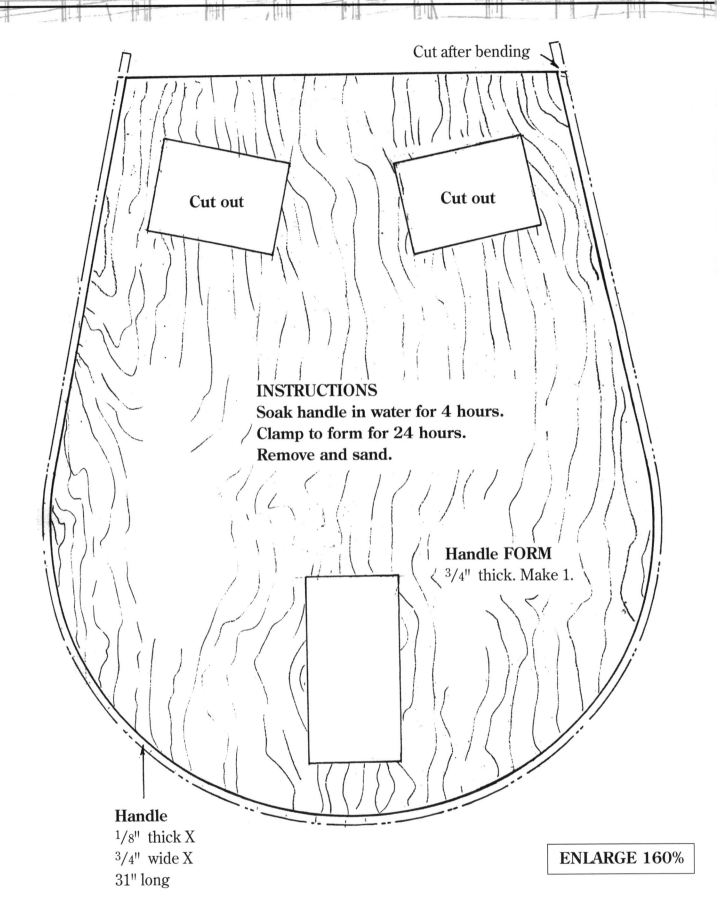

Cut after bending

Cut out

Cut out

**INSTRUCTIONS**
**Soak handle in water for 4 hours.**
**Clamp to form for 24 hours.**
**Remove and sand.**

**Handle FORM**
3/4" thick. Make 1.

**Handle**
1/8" thick X
3/4" wide X
31" long

ENLARGE 160%

# 8 The Julie Ann Basket

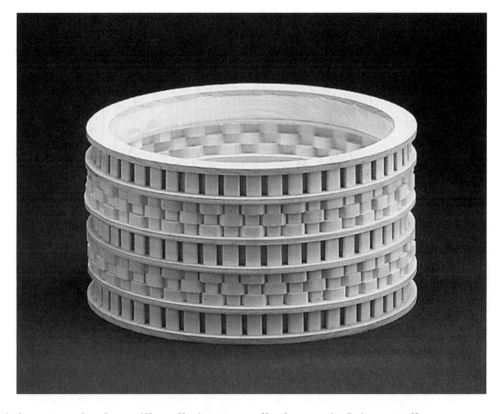

This round tight weave basket will really impress all who see it. It is actually easy to cut out and after it is assembled it looks very real. For contrast, apply a dark stain or use contrasting wood on the 4 spacers.

## Assembly View

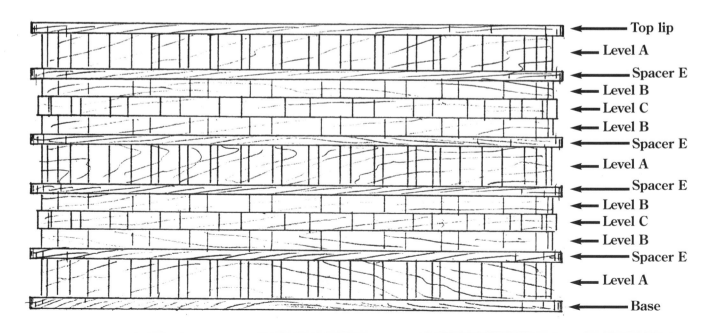

- Top lip
- Level A
- Spacer E
- Level B
- Level C
- Level B
- Spacer E
- Level A
- Spacer E
- Level B
- Level C
- Level B
- Spacer E
- Level A
- Base

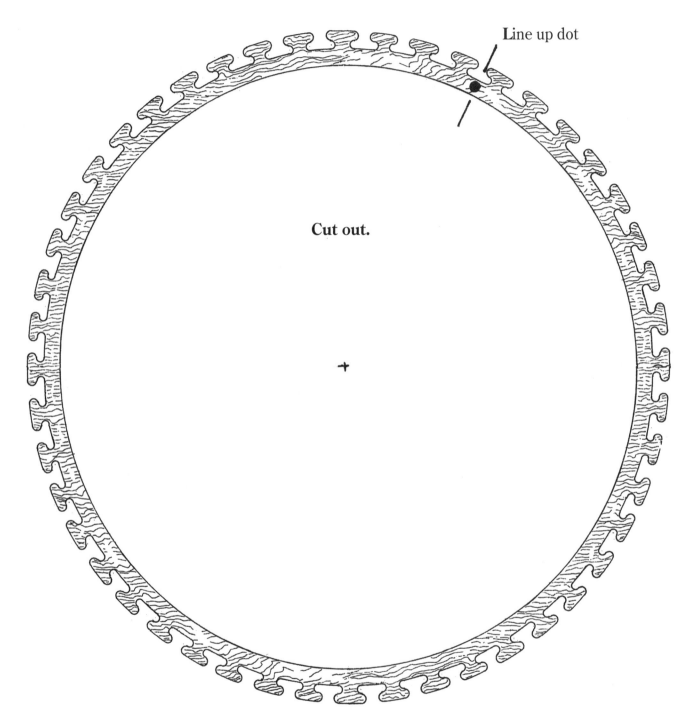

Line up dot

Cut out.

+

**Levels A—**$^1/_2''$ thick. Make 3.

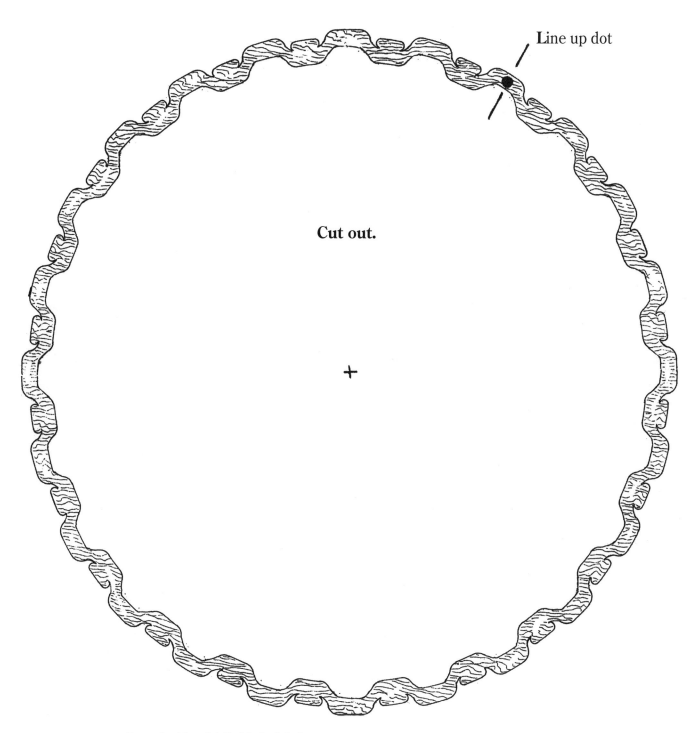

Line up dot

Cut out.

+

**Levels B**—1/4" thick. Make 4.

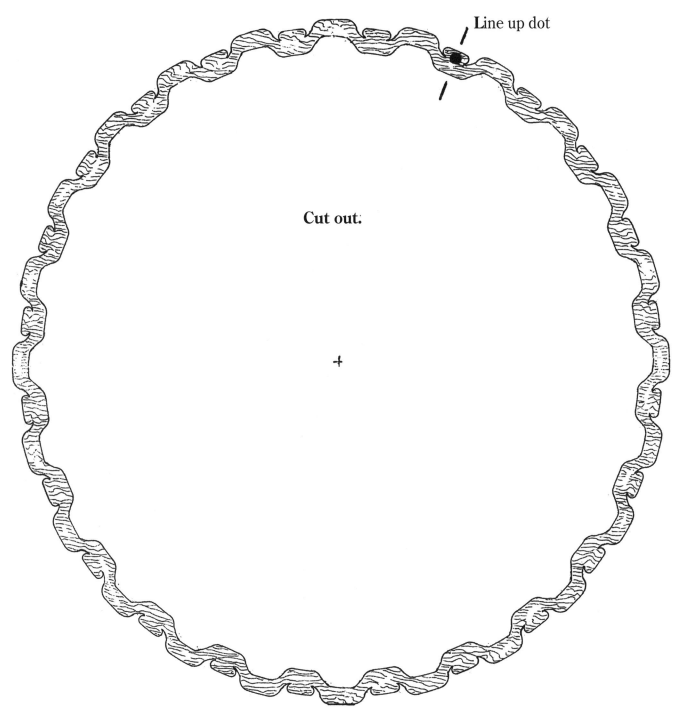

Line up dot

Cut out.

Levels C—1/4" thick. Make 2.

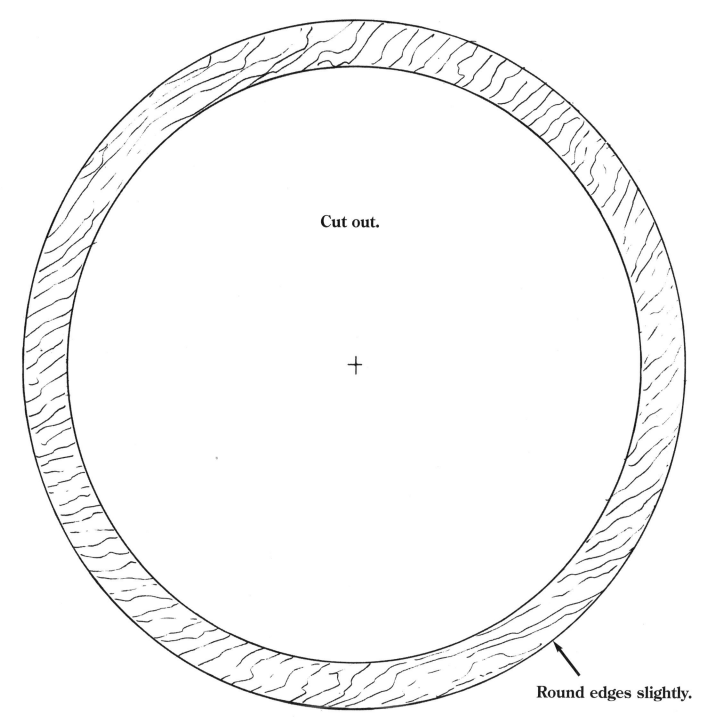

Cut out.

Round edges slightly.

**Top Lid/Level D**—$1/8''$ thick. Make 5.

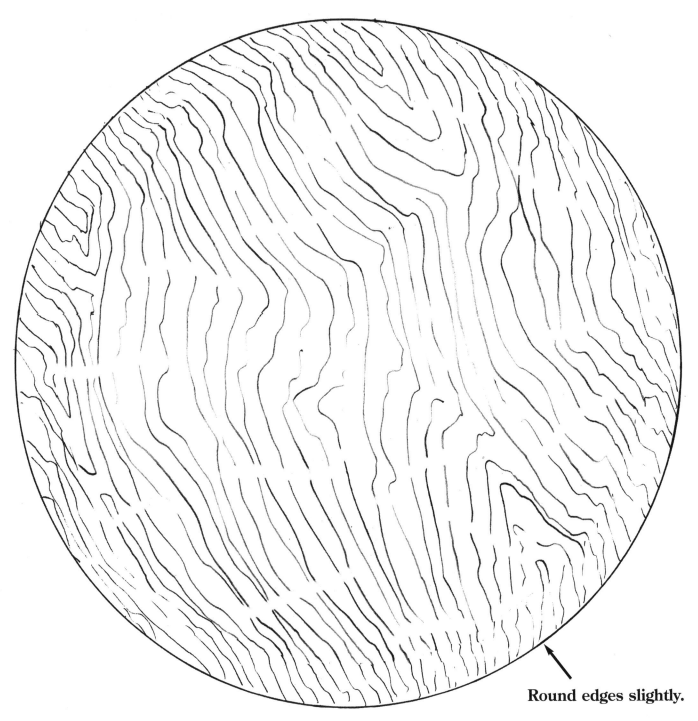

**Round edges slightly.**

**Base**—3/16" thick. Make 1.

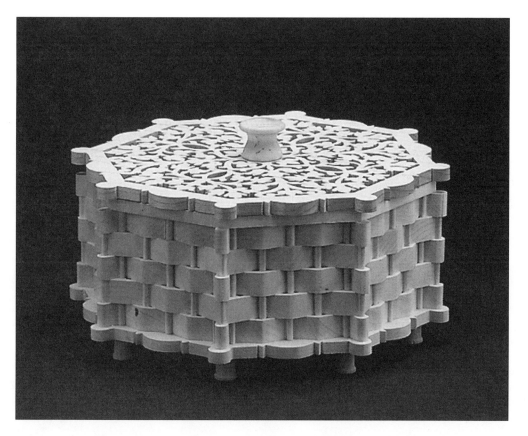

# 9 Victorian Bride Basket with Lid

**Assembly View**

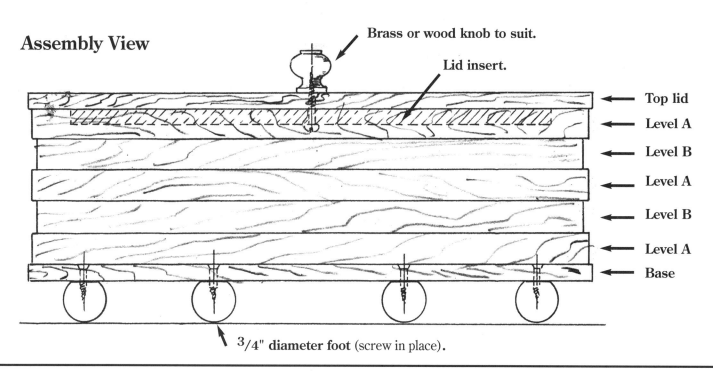

Brass or wood knob to suit.

Lid insert.

Top lid

Level A

Level B

Level A

Level B

Level A

Base

3/4" diameter foot (screw in place).

Line up dot.

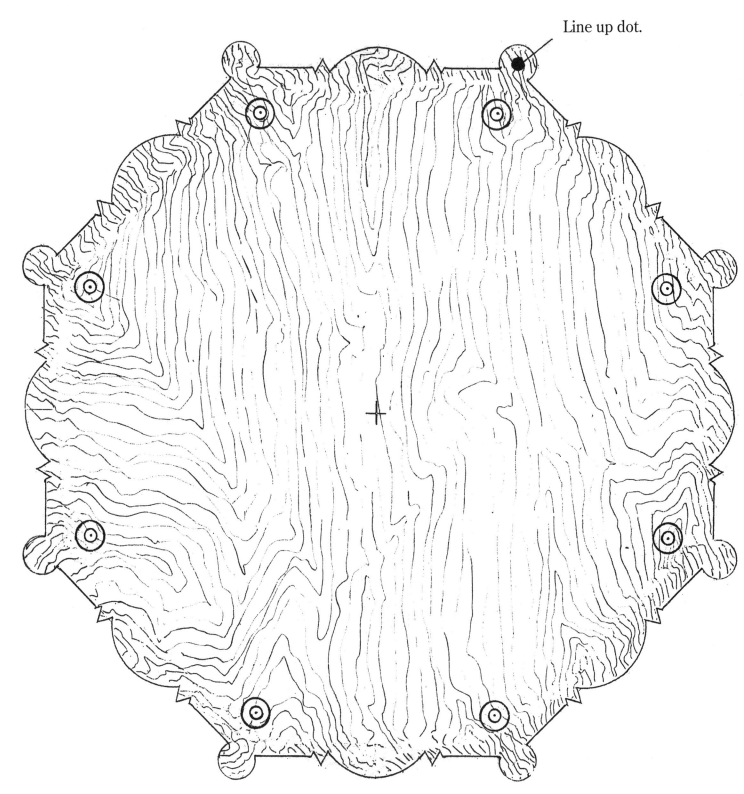

**Base**—1/4" thick. Make 1.

Line up dot.

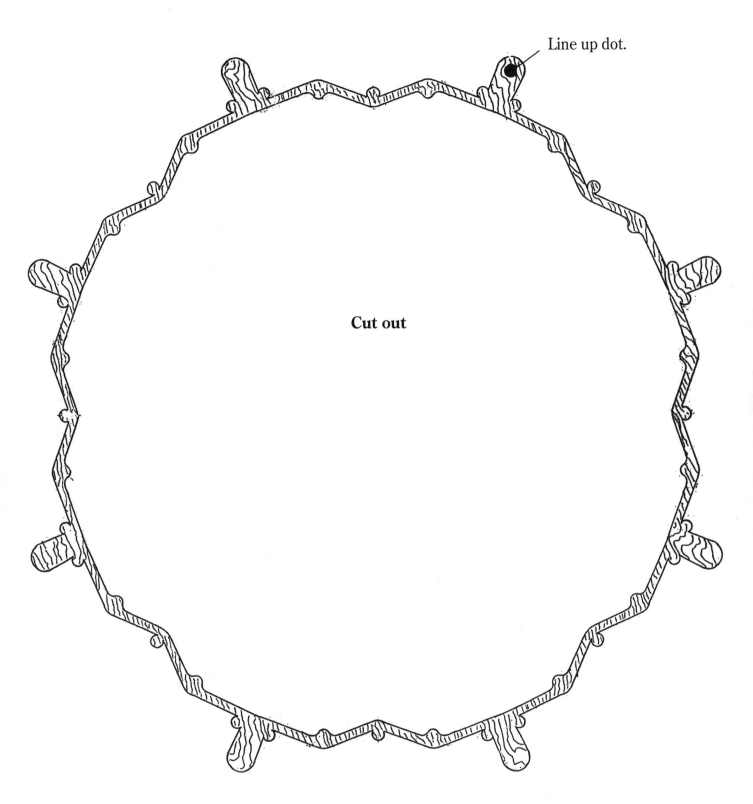

**Cut out**

**Level A**—1/2" thick. Make 3.

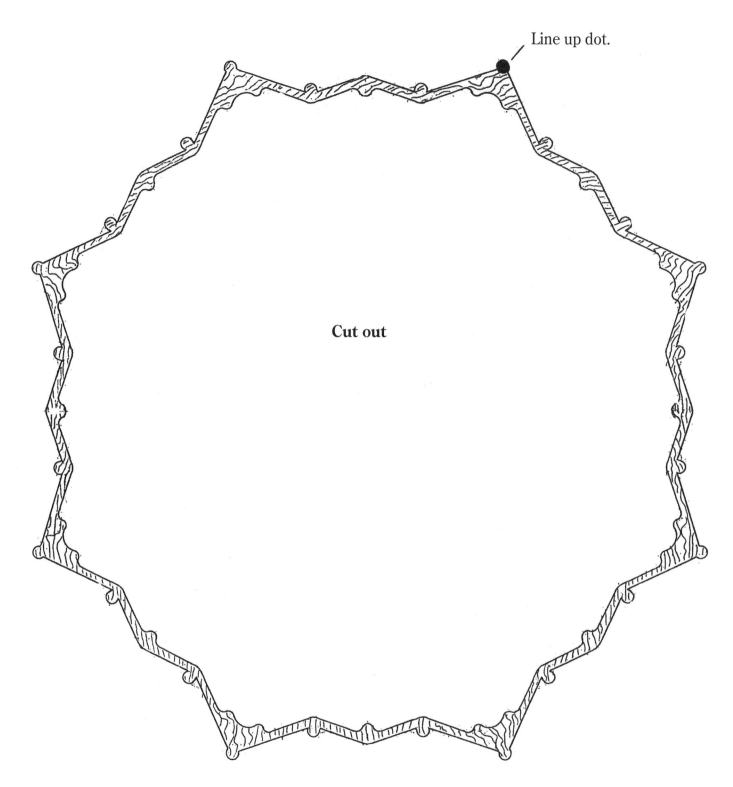

Line up dot.

Cut out

**Level B**—1/2" thick. Make 2.

Line up dot.

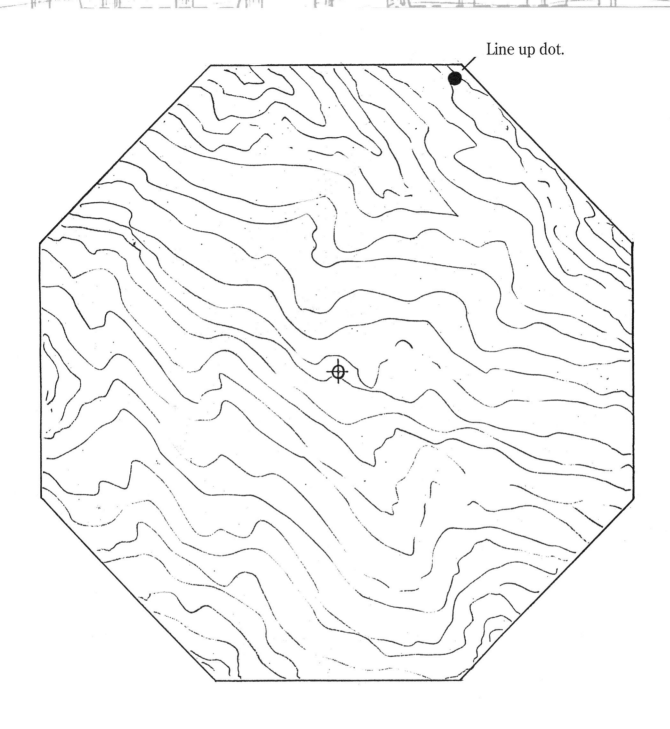

**Lid insert**—1/4″ thick. Make 1. (Dark stain.)

Line up dot.

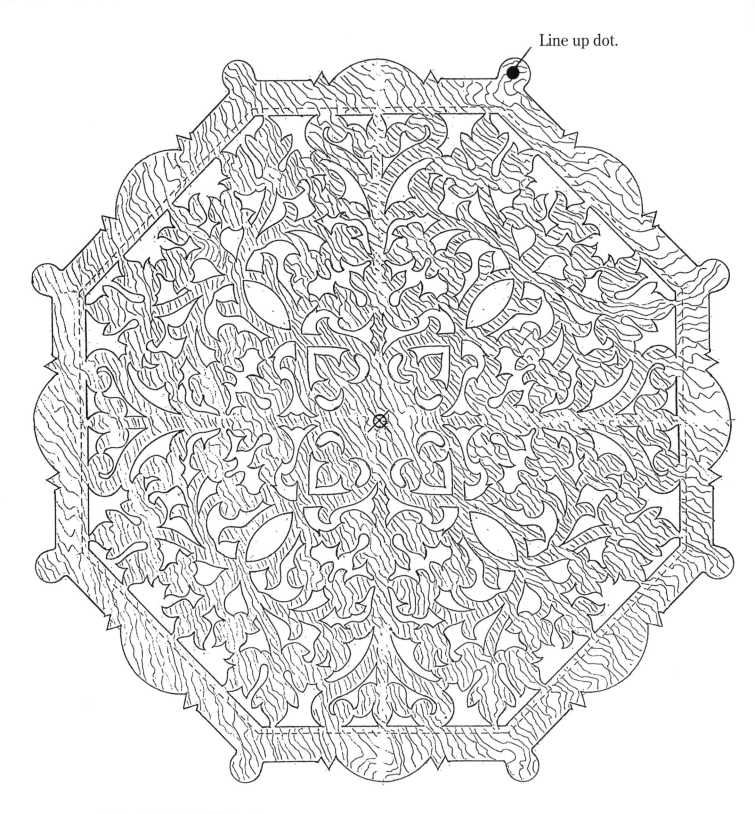

**Lid**—1/4" thick. Make 1.

# 10 Queen Anne Basket
## with eight sides

This basket is a copy of an original 1890 scroll saw basket with our new "weave"-effect added. The lid design was taken directly from the original antique.

Line up dot.

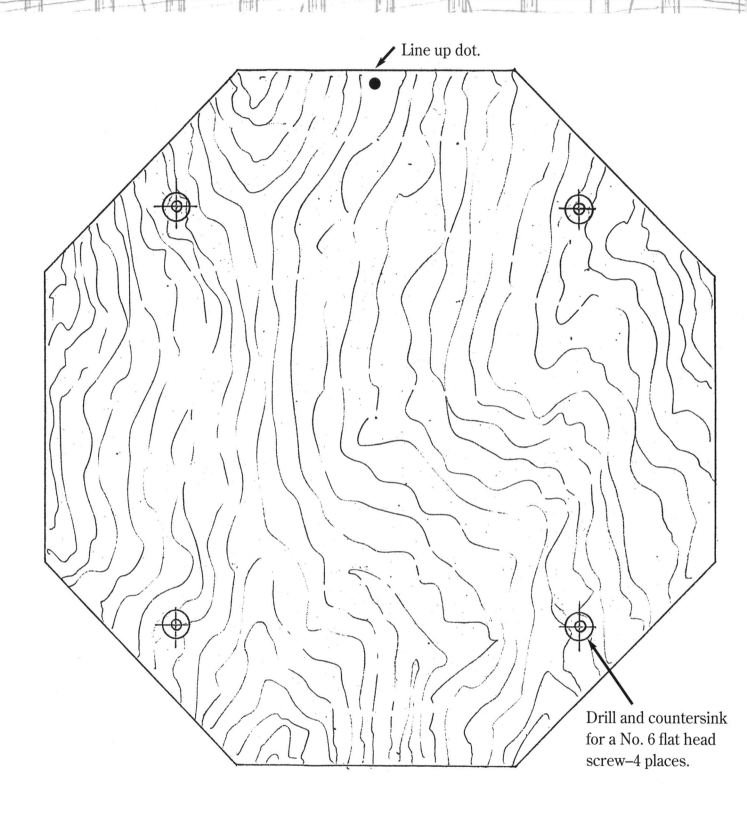

Drill and countersink
for a No. 6 flat head
screw–4 places.

**Base**—1/4" thick. Make 1.

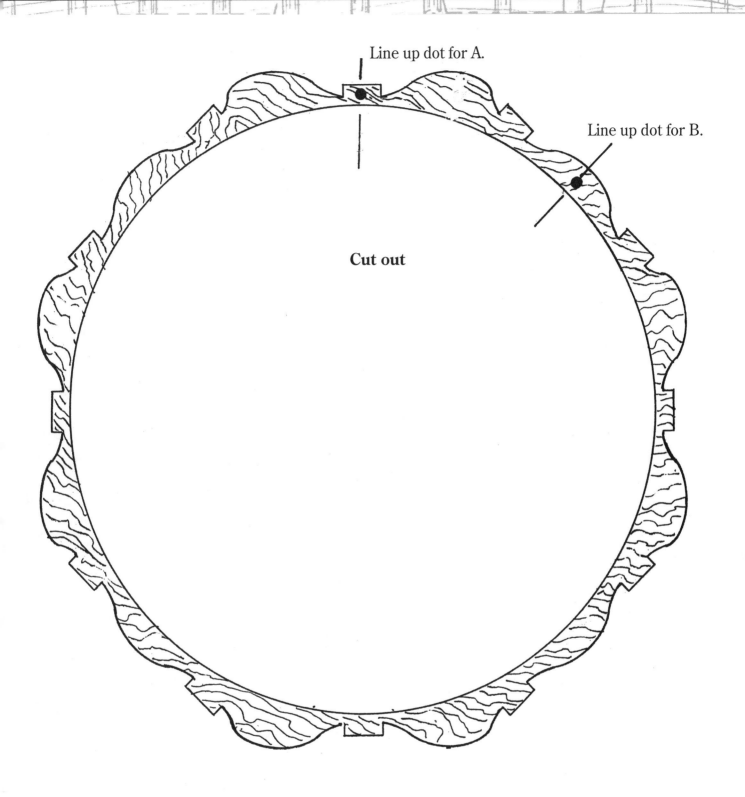

Line up dot for A.

Line up dot for B.

**Cut out**

**Level A/Level B**—$1/2$" thick. Make 6.

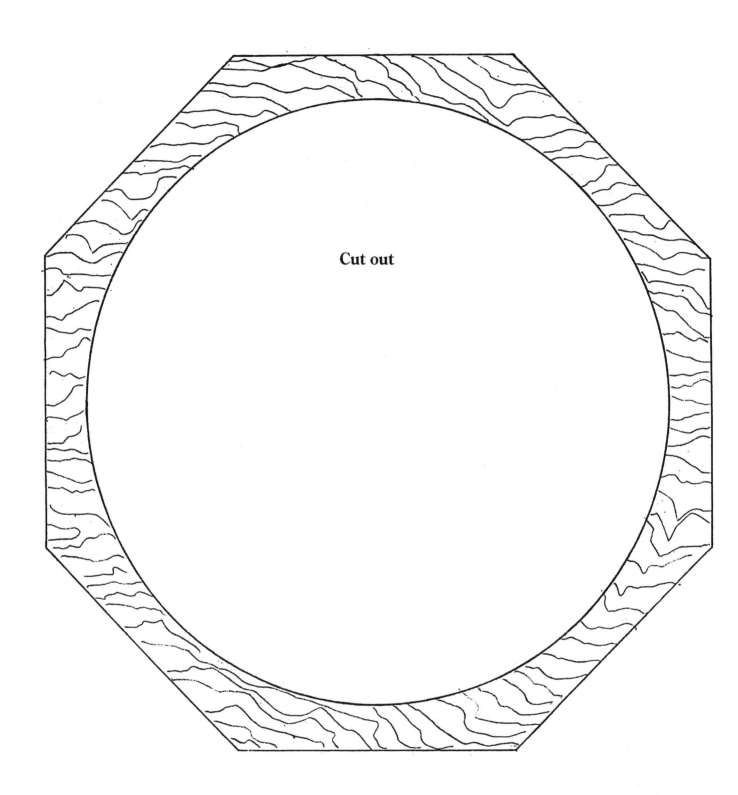

**Spacer**—1/8" thick. Make 1.

Dark stain for contrast.

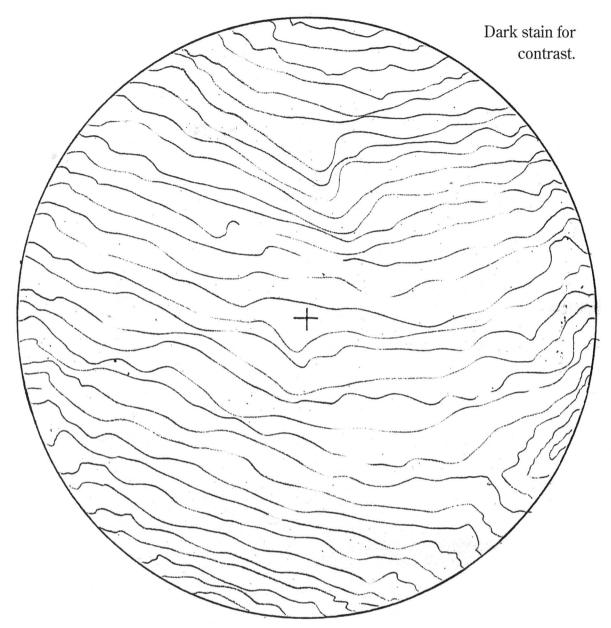

**Lid liner**—1/4" thick. Make 1.

**Handle**—1/4" thick. Make 1 of each.

**Lid**—1/4" thick. Make 1.

# 11 1880 New England Basket with Handle

This basket is a copy of an early original fretwork basket. It does not have a *weave* but it is a beautiful basket.

## Assembly View

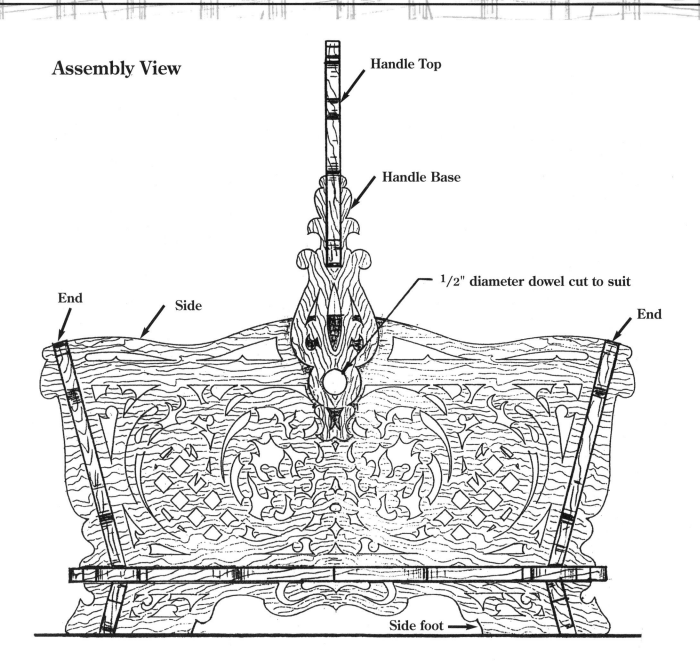

Handle Top

Handle Base

1/2" diameter dowel cut to suit

End

Side

End

Side foot

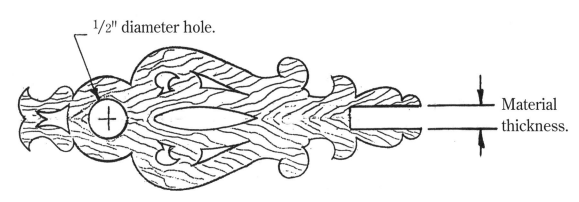

1/2" diameter hole.

Material thickness.

**Handle Base**—1/4" thick. Make 2.

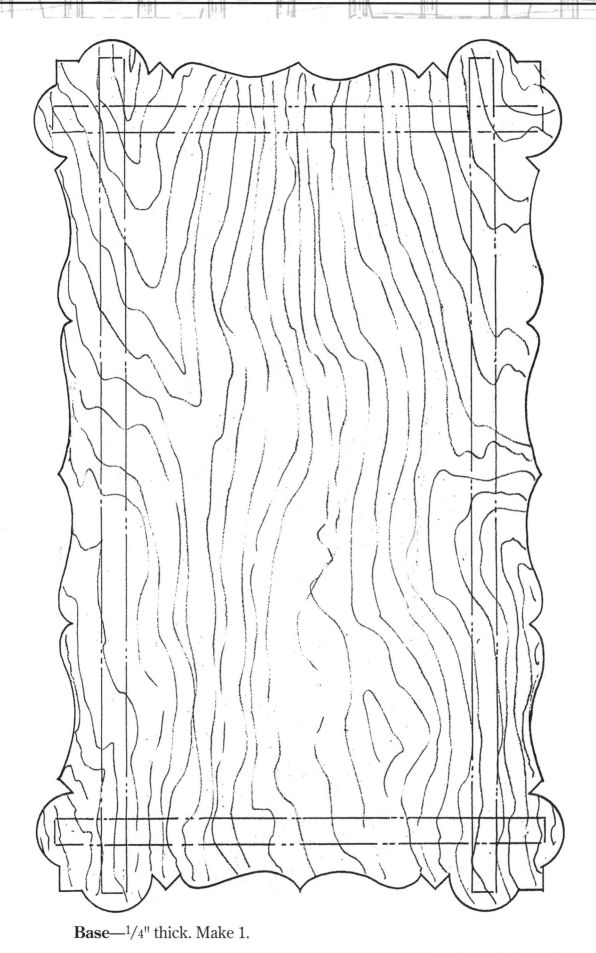

**Base**—1/4" thick. Make 1.

**1880 New England Basket with han-**

Material thickness.

**Side**—1/4" thick.
Make 2.

Cut at 5°.

**End View**—5°

**1880 New England Basket with handle**

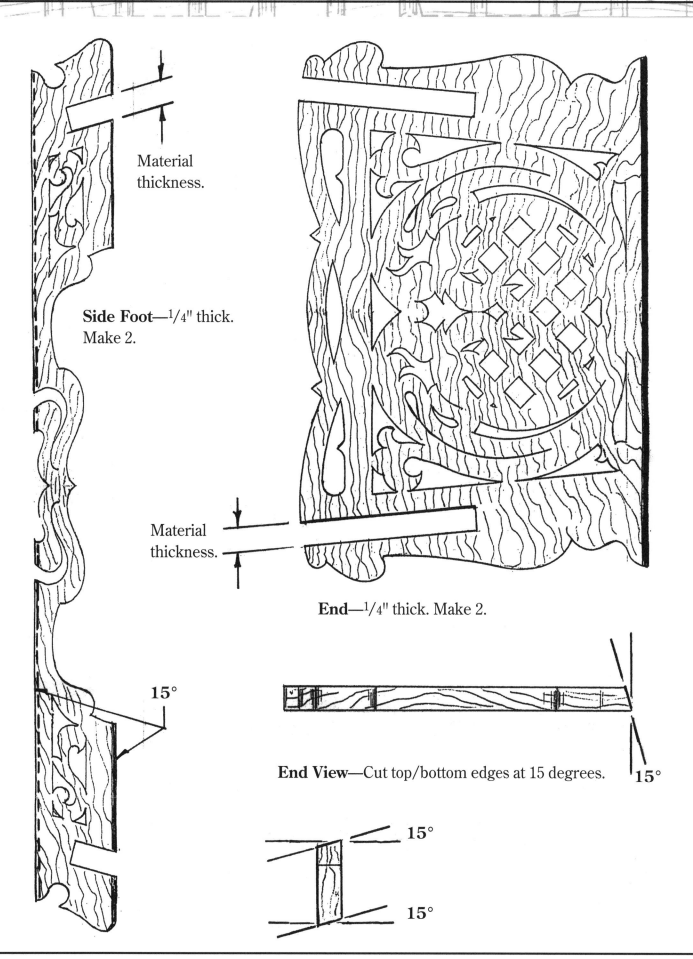

Material thickness.

**Side Foot**—1/4" thick. Make 2.

Material thickness.

**End**—1/4" thick. Make 2.

15°

**End View**—Cut top/bottom edges at 15 degrees.

15°

15°

15°

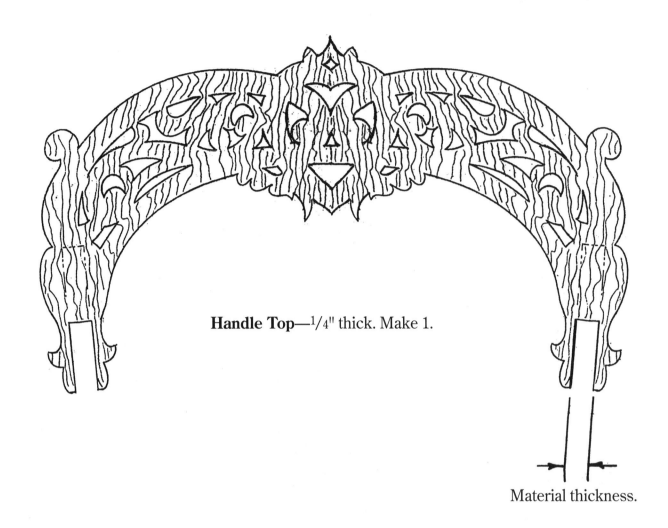

**Handle Top**—1/4" thick. Make 1.

Material thickness.

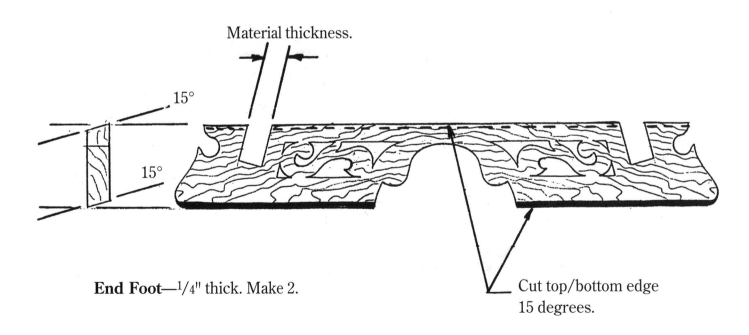

Material thickness.

15°

15°

**End Foot**—1/4" thick. Make 2.

Cut top/bottom edge
15 degrees.

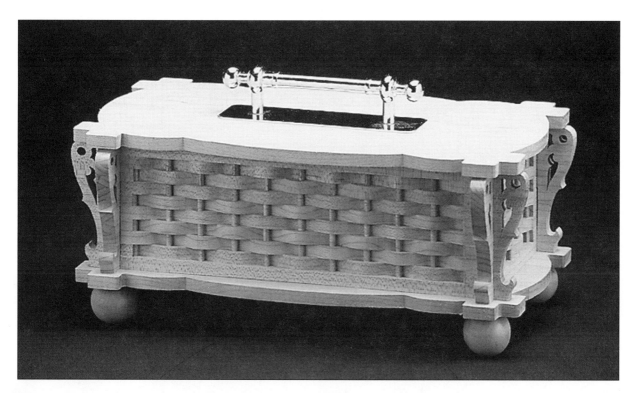

# 12 The Dublin Basket

This basket is made of scraps from all the first 12 baskets. It is made from scraps $1/4$ inch thick and $5/16$ inches wide pieces. A great way to use your scraps.

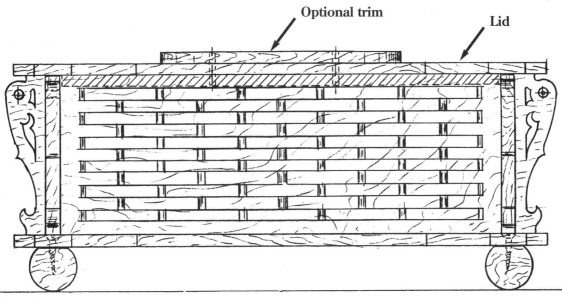

Optional trim

Lid

**Assembly View**

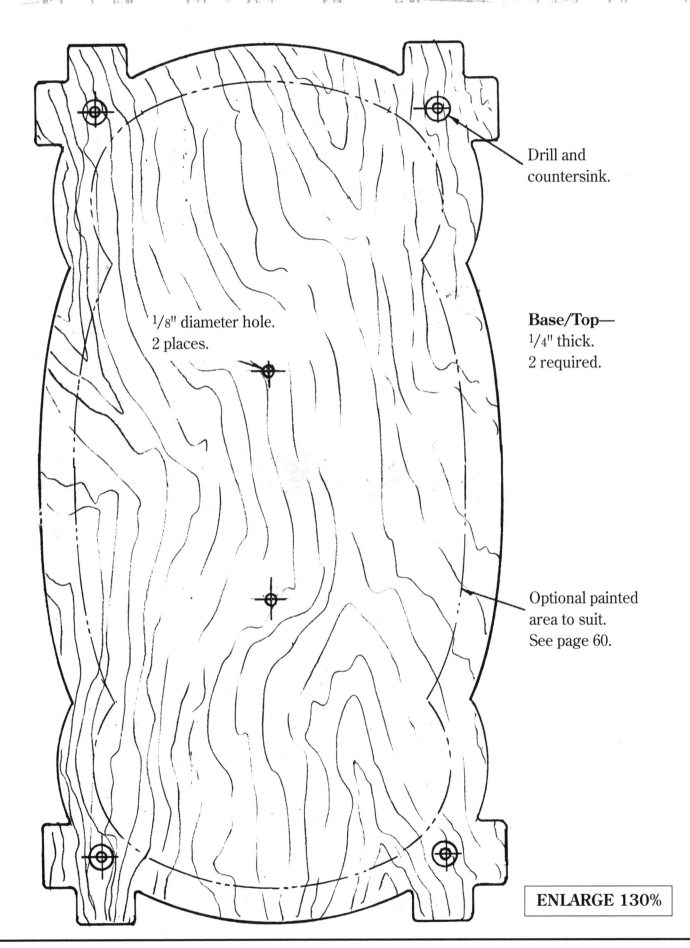

Drill and
countersink.

1/8" diameter hole.
2 places.

**Base/Top—**
1/4" thick.
2 required.

Optional painted
area to suit.
See page 60.

**ENLARGE 130%**

Pattern

**Cut to length—**
**12 1/8" and 7 1/8"**

Optional.
Stack cut 5 or 6
levels at a time.

1/4"

5/16"

12 1/8"

7 1/8"

Make
4 plain
1/4" x 5/16" x
12 1/8" pieces
and
4 plain
1/4" x 5/16" x
7 1/8" pieces

A—
make 12

B—
make 10

C—
make 12

D—
make 10

**ENLARGE 130%**

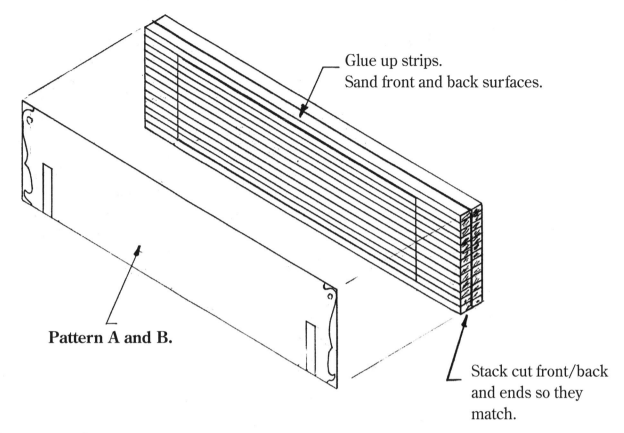

Glue up strips.
Sand front and back surfaces.

Pattern A and B.

Stack cut front/back
and ends so they
match.

## Instructions:

1. Cut up scrap wood into pieces $1/4$" thick by $5/16$" wide.

2. Cut these pieces into lengths of 7 $1/8$" and 12 $1/8$" in length. (You will need 20 - 7 $1/8$" long and 24 - 12 $1/8$" long).

3. Glue patterns A-B-C and D to the strips.

4. Cut out as required.

5. Glue the strips into pieces 3 $1/4$" x 7 $1/8$" and 3 $1/4$" x 12 $1/8$"; make two of each. Sand front and back surfaces.

6. Attach pattern A and pattern B to sides/ends.

7. Cut out. See above sketch. (You might want to stack cut the 2 pieces).

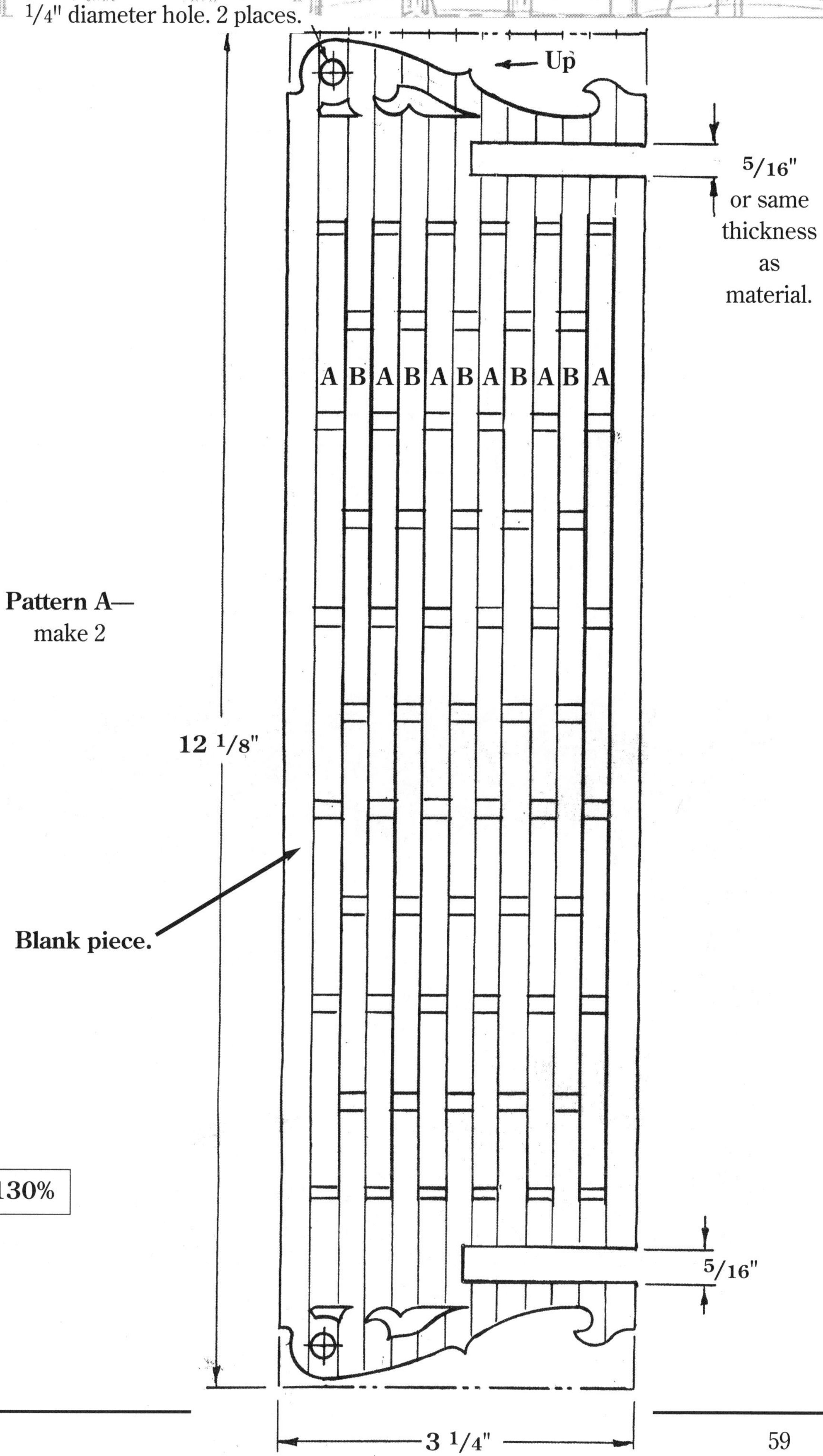

1/4" diameter hole. 2 places.

← Up

5/16"
or same
thickness
as
material.

A B A B A B A B A B A

**Pattern A—**
make 2

12 1/8"

Blank piece.

**ENLARGE 130%**

5/16"

3 1/4"

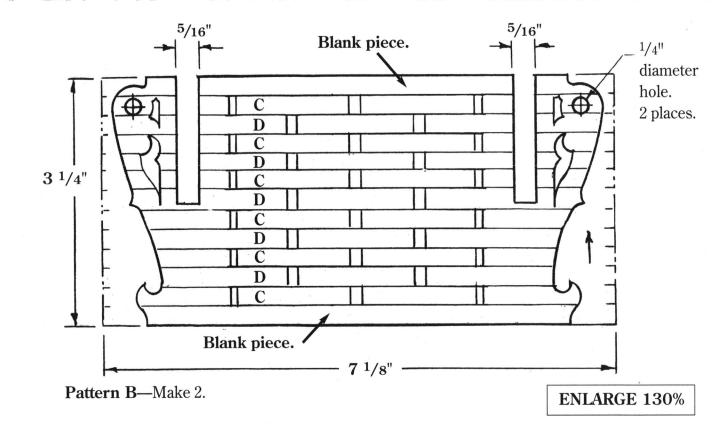

5/16"

Blank piece.

5/16"

1/4" diameter hole. 2 places.

3 1/4"

C
D
C
D
C
D
C
D
C
D
C

Blank piece.

7 1/8"

**Pattern B—Make 2.**

**ENLARGE 130%**

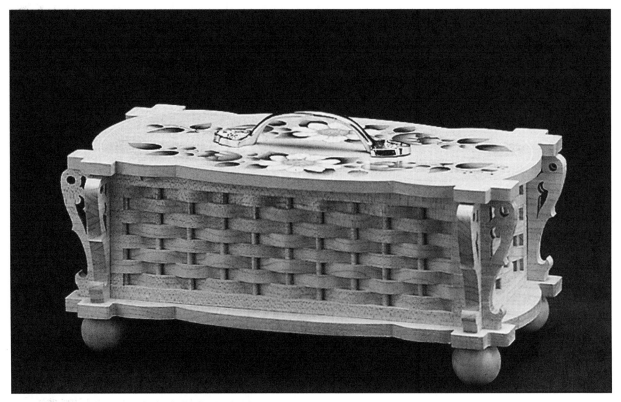

## OPTIONAL PAINTED LID

If you like tole painted projects, the lid on this basket will give you the opportunity to really display your tole painting talent. Tole painting really adds a lot to this basket.

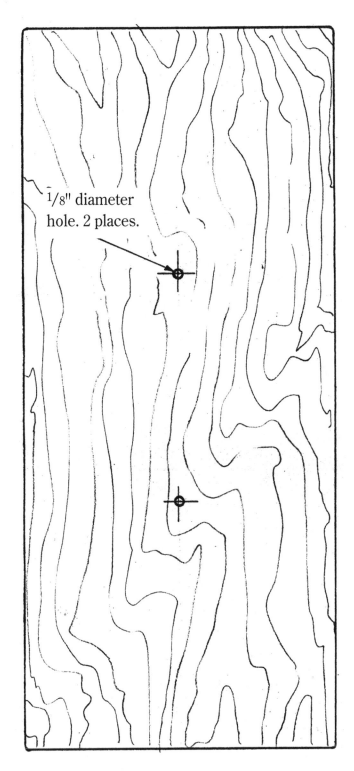

1/8" diameter hole. 2 places.

**Lid Guide**—1/4" thick. Make 1.

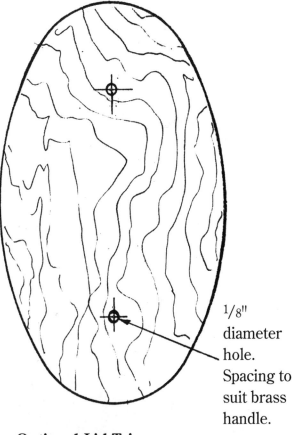

1/8" diameter hole. Spacing to suit brass handle.

**Optional Lid Trim—**
1/8" thick. Make 1.

**Recommended Handle—**
Klockit No. 38020 or equal.
Call 1-800-556-2548.

**Foot—**1" diameter. 4 required.

# John Nelson's
# First Scroll Saw Baskets Book

You will enjoy *Making Wooden Baskets on Your Scroll Saw*
by John Nelson and William Guimond.
The first book shows each step in the basketweave scroll saw process,
plus contains patterns for 12 different baskets.

64 pages, 8.5 x 11, $9.95

Available at your favorite supplier.

Direct orders (add $2.50 shipping):
Fox Book Orders
1970 Broad Street
East Petersburg, PA 17520